Jinny Johnson

Raccoon

Published by Smart Apple Media,
an imprint of Black Rabbit Books
P.O. Box 3263, Mankato, Minnesota, 56002
www.blackrabbitbooks.com

Printed in the United States of America,
at Corporate Graphics in North Mankato, Minnesota.

Designed by Hel James
Edited by Mary-Jane Wilkins

Cataloging-in-Publication Data
is available from the Library of Congress

ISBN 978-1-62588-036-9

Photo acknowledgements
t = top, b = bottom
title page Hemera/Thinkstock; page 3 iStockphoto/Thinkstock;
4 Heiko Kiera/Shutterstock; 5 Gerald A. DeBoer/Shutterstock;
7 iStockphoto/Thinkstock; 8 Aistov Alexey/Thinkstock;
9 samodelkin8/Shutterstock; 10 BMJ/Shutterstock; 11 Hemera/
Thinkstock; 12, 13, 14, 15 iStockphoto/Thinkstock; 16 Evoken/
Shutterstock; 17 Christian Colista/Shutterstock; 18 Denise Kappa/
Shutterstock; 19 iStockphoto/Thinkstock; 20 iStockphoto/
Thinkstock, 22t worldswildlifewonders, b Rozhkovs/both
Shutterstock; 23 Melody Mulligan/Shutterstock
Cover iStockphoto/Thinkstock

DAD0509
052013
9 8 7 6 5 4 3 2 1

Contents

I'm a raccoon.

I'm happy living almost anywhere, but somewhere with trees and water suits me best.

First Days

My three brothers and I were born
in our mom's den in a hole in a tree.
We were tiny and helpless but our mom
took good care of us. She fed us with her milk.

When we were about nine
weeks old we peeked out
of our den for the first time.

Then we started to play and explore.
Everything was new and exciting.

Growing Up

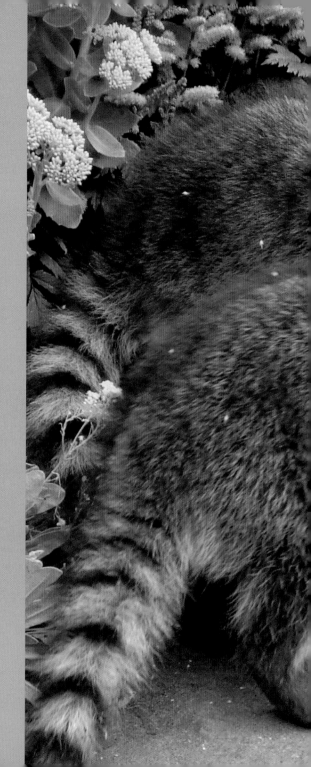

We quickly learned how to find our own food. By the time we were about 20 weeks old we could feed ourselves, with no help from mom.

We stayed close to our mom until we were almost a year old, though. Little raccoons like us have to watch out for predators such as owls and snakes.

My Furry Coat

Like all raccoons I have black markings
across my eyes like a bandit's mask.
This makes me look very rascally!

My tail is bushy with dark rings around it.
The rest of my fur is gray, but some raccoons
have brownish or almost black fur.

Paws and Teeth

My hands look quite like yours and I have five fingers on each hand. My feet are slightly larger and I can sit up on my back legs when I want to.

I have about 40 sharp teeth so I can
eat most kinds of food. I usually pick
up my food in my front paws before
putting it into my mouth.

My Favorite Foods

I'm not fussy
about my food.

Raccoons eat lots of fruit, nuts, and grain.
We like eggs too and we catch insects,
crayfish, frogs, and other small creatures.

We're also happy to search your trash can for any food you've thrown away. Yum!

My Day

During the day I generally take it easy
and stay close to home. I wake up in
the evening and go off in search of food.

I have good hearing and I can see well in the dark—

—very useful when you're a night-time hunter.

15

On the Move

I'm quick on my feet. I can run at up to 15 miles an hour (24 km/h) if I have to, although I prefer not to travel too far for my food.

I also climb well and like to make my den in a tree if possible.

I will even swim to find a good meal. But my fur isn't waterproof, so I'd rather stay out of water.

Clever Creatures

Some people say that raccoons are the most mischievous of all animals. I'd say that we're very clever.

We're good with our hands and we can open jars and untie knots.

Some of us like living near humans. We know you always have food around.

My Own Family

I'm a year old now and soon I will find a mate and have cubs of my own.

I'll make a warm den in a tree or cave, or even in an old building where I can keep my cubs safe.

I will feed them with my milk for about 10 weeks until they are ready to start eating other foods.

Raccoon Facts

Raccoons belong to a family of mammals that also includes ringtails. Raccoons live all over North and Central America and have also been introduced to parts of Asia and Europe.

An average raccoon is about 20 inches (50 cm) long with a 12-inch (32 cm) tail. It weighs about 15 pounds (10 kg). Females are slightly smaller and lighter.

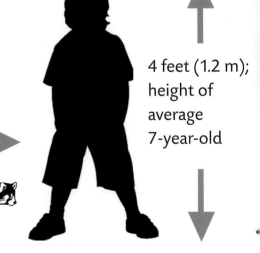

4 feet (1.2 m)

4 feet (1.2 m); height of average 7-year-old

These animals will live almost anywhere, including near humans in towns and cities. They make dens in old buildings and lofts and are very happy to eat food thrown away by humans.

Useful Words

den The home of an animal such as a raccoon. The den is usually underground.

predator An animal that lives by hunting and killing other animals.

Index

Web Link

Learn more about raccoons at: http://kids.nationalgeographic.co.uk/kids/animals/creaturefeature/raccoon/